ISBN 978-0-656-34104-7

PIBN 10796113

RELIQUES

OF

THE CHRIST

BY

DENIS WORTMAN, D.D

Ἡ βασιλεία τοῦ Θεοῦ ἐντὸς ὑμῶν ἐστιν

NEW YORK

E. P. DUTTON & COMPANY

31 WEST TWENTY-THIRD STREET

1888

Press of J. J. Little & Co.
Astor Place, New York.

TO

MY DEAR WIFE,

JESSIE BABCOCK WORTMAN,

𝔍𝔫 𝔥𝔦𝔰 𝔑𝔞𝔪𝔢.

RELIQUES OF THE CHRIST.

I.

I WONDER if in Nazareth,
  By heedless feet o'errun,
There lingers still some dear relique
  Of work by Joseph's Son;
Some carvèd thought, some tool of toil,
  Some house with stones grown gray,
A home He built who had not where
  His weary head to lay.

It were a thing most beautiful,
　Of rare and rich design;
And something very true and strong,
　Made by a skill divine;
The road-side stones at sight of Him
　Could scarce their rapture hush;
What felt his touch and art must yet
　With conscious beauty blush.

I visit Nazareth, ask each man,
　Each mound, each stone, each wind;
" I pray ye, help some precious trace
　Of your great Builder find; "
Alas! ye listeners to my plaint,
　The startled silence saith:
" What once was false, is now too true—
　No Christ in Nazareth! "

But, O my soul, why thus cast down?
　　A truer Nazareth scan;
What if thou find no time-spoiled work
　　Of Christ, the Son of Man?—
Joy yet to thee; lift up thy head,
　　Cast raptured gaze abroad,
See in this vast Christ-builded world
　　Signs of the Son of God.

So Nazareth may silent be,
　　But earth shall have her song;
And all things true and beautiful,
　　And all things grand and strong,
And very humblest, too, shall sing:
　　" Through Him have all things been;
And without Him was nothing made:
　　Praise ye the Lord!　Amen."

How sacred all things now ! behold,
   The sun more brightly gleams,
The night with softer quietude
   And gentler radiance beams :
The wandering winds tone down their
Weird notes to soothing lays,   [wild,
   The ocean's waves tumultuous leap,
Lifting their voice in praise.

The skies wave lordlier banner-clouds,
   Fair fruits more savory seem,
The flowers breathe daintier fragrances,
   Wild wastès with verdure teem ;
The beauty is Christ's handiwork,
   The light glows from his face,
The perfume is his spirit ; all
   Earth's sweetness is his grace.

Ah ! Lovè is wisest alchemist,
    And Faith the truest test ;
By it bright Love discovers oft
    In very worst a best ;
From bitterness extracts a sweet,
    And, by fond joy enticed,
She cameos out from flinted griefs
    Choice keepsakes of the Christ.

II.

And so I tell thee, O my soul,
    I'll tell it to the earth :
If Christ have given thee his grace,
    Thou hast right cause for mirth ;
Thou art thyself such rare relique
    Of Godlike wit and love,
As hideth not in depths below,
    Or lighteth heights above.

For thy defence bald mountains stand
 And bare their breasts to storms,
The valleys are thy vassal slaves;
 Behold their prostrate forms!
Swift winds and waves thy chariots are,
 Sun, moon, and stars arise
To give thee light; to give thee life;
 Lo! the Incarnate dies.

O soul of mine! I tell thee true,
 If Christ indeed be thine,
Not more made He himself thy kin
 Than makes He thee divine:
As through his soul there frequent beat
 Our human hopes and loves,
So 'midst thy varying joys and fears
 His spirit lives and moves.

An Olive in Gethsemane
    Sometimes thou fain would'st be,
Roots watered, branches nourished by
    That blood-sweat shed for thee ;
Lo, by thy gnarlèd roots He groans
    Who feeds thy life with blood ;
And through thy spirit-veins distils
    The rich love-life of God.

Judean air thou fain would'st be,
    That to Christ's sacred kiss
Thou too mightst quiver, and to men
    Repeat his words of bliss ;
And all around a ruined world
    Of wrath and strife and woe,
Thine echoes of its full reprieve
    Should never cease their flow.

Be thou such Christ-breathed air, my soul,
　　As lightsome and as free,
As pure, and soft, and sensitive
　　To all He telleth thee ;
With gentlest brèezes fan his brow,
　　Love's fragrance to Him bear,
Waft round the earth his words of grace,
　　And heavenward lift his prayer.

III.

What reverent soul loves not to tread
　　The soil of Palestine,
And breathe the air, and kiss the sod,
　　Where his worn feet have been ?
Kneel in the mountains where He prayed,
　　Traverse the storm-calm'd sea,
Weep in the garden, bear some cross
　　To sacred Calvary ?

But O my soul, as I thy good
    And evil ways explore,
I seem to see the Christ in thee
    His earthly life live o'er,
Thou art another Holy Land,
    (Ah, holy mightst thou be !)
The olden joys and griefs of Christ
    Repeat themselves in thee.

No longing for his coming,
    No greeting Him with scorn,
No mountain for his praying,
    No sea by tempest torn,
No cheer of friends, nor wrath of foes,
    From manger to the tree,
But finds its faithful counterpart,
    Mysterious heart, in thee.

Thou art that Manger where we see
　　The infant Christ recline ;
The living, throbbing, human breast,
　　Nursing the Babe divine ;
Thy low-born thoughts the cattle are;
　　Thy high, the Magi wise :
Lo, o'er thee singing angels bend
　　And thrill with praise the skies.

Thou art that long-sought Nazarene work,
　　On which with love-taught skill
The Carpenter who is about
　　His Father's business still,
Doth toil through sunshine and through
　　And far into the night,　　[storm,
Building a house most beautiful
　　To crown some holy height.

Thou art that Temple where the Lord
    Out-teacheth scribes of law,
Whence afterward with cords He makes
    Coarse mammon-priests withdraw ;
Thine inmost court, a holy place,
    The Lord's own glory-home, .
Thine outer sentencing Him oft
    To shame and martyrdom.

Thou art most fair, Gennessaret
    With holy depths of calm,
Thy smile is heaven's portraiture,
    Thy breath a tender psalm :
Oh! who could guess such rageful storms
    Might spoil thy bright expanse ?
Who think o'er such sweet lyre* of God
    Might thrum such dissonance ?

        * Gennessaret—a lyre.

But wot thou well, my soul, of One
Who can thy rage control ;
Of One who sails serene the sea
When waves of wildness roll ;
The Master speaks—the maniac winds
Pause, listening to his will ;
Then all thy depths of calm return—
As He saith : " Peace, be still."

Thou art that upper chamber where
The Saviour is the guest ;
Where Judas a vile treason hides,
But John leans on his breast ;
Here breaketh he the mystic bread,
Here poureth mystic wine,
And in a human breast pours forth
A prayer, a love, divine.

Thou art the Garden, where the Christ
  Perchance hath oft essayed
Sweet hours of rest in solitude
  Beneath thine olive shade ;
Yet, oh, that blood-sweat, oh, that deep,
  That bitter agony
Of our dear Lord ! my soul, thou art
  His dark Gethsemane !

" Father, if it be possible,
  Let this cup pass from me ! "
My soul, that pleading prayer to God
  Was made in truth to thee ;
Thou would'st not make it possible ;
  " Not my will, then, but thine ! "
Thou hast thy way ; but, cruel soul,
  What sin hast thou made mine !

What, wilful soul, was Calvary's Cross
    But thine uplifted pride;
What saw thine angered sin so pierced
    His hands, his feet, his side?
Ay, what his thirst but for thy love?
    And had the Saviour's heart
So missed the Father hadst thou but
    Fulfilled the brother's part?

Lord, pardon me! love cannot be
    By Thee misunderstood;
These nails and spear are tokens dear
    They tell me of thy blood;
E'en from my sins my spirit wins
    This tender, reverent thought;
Through sins of mine, by sufferings thine
    Was my redemption wrought.

But, O my soul, I charge thee well,
  Reliques more noble gain
Than those which jeopardize thy life,
  And give the Lord such pain ;
Where be thy tears of penitence,
  Thine inward groans and sighs,
Thy restful trust, thy weeping love,
  Thy quick self-sacrifice ?

Dear Lord, the crucifier would
  Be crucified by Thee ;
Turn Thou thy love to instruments
  Of torture sweet to me !
Thrice welcome, cross and nail and spear !
  Oh, joy of agony !
I pardon Him that slayeth me,
  Pierced by his love, I die !

More precious now than wooden cross
   The crosses daily borne ;
Than thorns of old, the griefs by which
   The heart's self-love is torn ;
Sacred as Calvary's mournful road.
   The rough paths daily trod ;
But best of all, or cross, or crown,
   As pleaseth Thee, my God !

So this I say, my soul, as I
   Thy devious ways explore ;
I seem to see the Christ in thee
   His earthly life live o'er ;
Thou art another Holy Land—
   (Ah, holy mightst thou be !)
The olden joys and griefs of Christ
   Repeat themselves in thee.

No longing for his coming,
  No greeting him with scorn,
No mountain for his praying,
  No sea by tempest torn;
No cheer of friend, no wrath of foe,
  From manger to the tree,
But finds its faithful counterpart,
  Mysterious heart, in thee!

IV.

I wonder hath the World a heart
  Her Master's pangs to know;
I wonder hath she yet forgot
  That sweet and tender woe;
I wonder if her soul doth not
  Yet quiver with the pain
That throbbed with earthquake violence
  When gentle Christ was slain!

Oh, it is beautiful to think,
    That God hath well decreed
A certain great undyingness
    To live in every deed ;
A world's unrest, an insect's flight
    Is felt by furthest star ;
And all our works and words and
    Like us, immortal are.   [thoughts,

And sure, if the great World-Heart notes
    The evening insect-hum,
Of Calvary's plaintive psalm it ne'er
    Forgetful shall become ;
If Nature minds the pressure slight
    Of erring human feet,
What thrill when Jesus trod her plains !
    The memory, how sweet !

No need we fondly traverse back
 The ancient centuries through,
That with Jerusalem's wondering throng
 We may see Jesus too ;
O eyes so blind ! O ears so deaf
 To this great teaching list !
The wide world echoes endlessly
 With that strange life of Christ.

Lo, all the air is tremulous
 With his sweet words of grace,
The rhythmic hints of God-like speech
 In these wild winds we trace ;
Still in her rocky heart Earth hears
 The echo of his tread,
And listens with a mute delight
 To all the Master said.

Lo, all the air, so tremulous

    With his sweet words of grace,

Still pulsates with the radiance

    Of his love-lucent face ;

And the vast ether-world, that bears

    The news from sun to sun,

Bids all its myriad wingèd steeds

    On this new errand run.

Lo ! all the ether-firmament

   · Yet quivers in amaze,

And will not from the Christ-life draw

    Its reverential gaze ;

Now worlds afar that life behold,

    Yes—they the Christ may see,

And gaze in sweet, sad wonderment

    On sad, sweet Calvary !

No wonder, with such news to bear,
  So swift thou art, O Light!
No wonder, Earth, thy daily turn
  To show all worlds the sight;
No wonder, now, while we below
  Are shrouded in our night,
That ye, O vision-favored Spheres,
  Shine forth so glad, so bright!

Ah, Worlds, ye cannot shine too bright,
  Nor sing too joyously,
Nor up your infinite highways
  March too triumphantly;
And some day God may give me leave
  To go where the visions shine,
And the sight of the Lord and all He did
  Shall then, my soul, be thine!

And gay and quick as humming-birds
  Dart 'mong the flowerets fair,
Shall be thy rapturous, flashing flight
  From radiant star to star ;
Nor such a feast to humming-bird
  May daintiest honey be,
As each fresh view of Jesus' life
  Shall be, my soul, to thee.

O Bethlehem ! O Bethlehem !
  We'll hear thy choirs again,
" Glory to God on high ! on earth
  Peace, and good will to men !"
The countless peoples of the skies
  Shall seize the uplifted song,
And ages over ages pour
  The tidal psalm along.

Glad City of the angel-song,

  Not *one* star then shall come

To bow in solitary pause

  O'er thy blest manger-home ;

Lo, then fulfilled the Patriarch's dream,

  And none shall envious be,

As sun and moon and all the stars

  Obeisance make to thee !

Then, Worlds, ye cannot shine too bright,

  Nor sing too joyously,

Nor up your infinite highways

  March too triumphantly ;

And some day God shall give me leave

  To go where the visions shine ;

The sight of the Lord and all He did

  Shall, raptured soul, be thine !

But O, ye far-off Times, is all
    Your mighty wondrousness
But echo and sad spectacle
    Of earth's strange wantonness,
That slew great Christ and buried him
    Out of its sight and love?
Oh, hath Christ died so utterly
    Nor lives somewhere above;

Somewhere above the lowlands damp
    Of mournful, shaded earth;
Somewhere above these poor misthoughts
    Of human hearted birth ;
Somewhere above the solemn heights
    Of utmost sentinel star ;
The living, loving, crownèd Christ,
    In his august Somewhere?

V.

There is a City great and strong,
　　Twelve gates of precious stones,
With turrets and high battlements,
　　Not needing light of suns ;
The streets aglow with fire of gold,
　　It hath no sound of strife ;
In glory all its own it stands
　　Beside the stream of Life.

A joy is there that knows no cloy,
　　A light that ne'er grows dim,
A multitude that never cease
　　From grateful praise and hymn ;
Lo, all the sainted sons of earth,
　　And angels there I view ;
And there, O vision glorious,
　　There standeth Jesus too !

Jesus, I know 'tis He ; I see
   The mark of nail and spear ;
And on his face I catch the trace
   Of earth-time smile and tear ;
But on his brow a crown shines now,
   And bending hosts adore !
'Tis He, 'tis He who on the tree
   The thorn-crown meekly wore !

O wondrous-fair Jerusalem,
   Shall I thy gates pass through ?
Thy jubilations surely join,
   Thy lordly splendors view ?
O Crucified, O Glorified,
   Shall I thy face behold,
And join the ransomed as they sing
   Along the streets of gold ?

Ah, Time, forgotten now thy toils,
  Thy cares and sins and tears ;
To my enraptured vision, lo !
  The eternal home appears ;
And through the Father's palaces
  I shall ecstatic rove,
Nor weary ever as I sing
  Emmanuel's grace and love.

O Crowns and Thrones and Sapphires,
  Ye glisten in the light !   [how
Ye cannot flash too far your joy,
  Ye cannot blaze too bright ;
And some day God shall bid me dwell
  Where the great visions shine,
The sight of the Lord and all he is
  Shall be the world's and mine.

Thou wondrously fair City, what

    Can mean thy dazzling light?

And what thy golden pavements broad?

    Thy singers robed in white?

What mean thy walls bejewelled, what

    Thy gates of pearl so strong;

Now thine impressive silences,

    Now thy far-sounding song?

VI.

A dream! The City of the Christ

    And that of Love are one;

For each the fairest is, and best

    The sons of God have known;

They are the one broad sovereignty,

    They have the one high throne,

And Christ ne'er is where Love rules not,

    From furthest zone to zone.

Love is a city, wall'd and tower'd,
  With bulwarks builded high,
On every foe they rise to frown,
  And foolish passer-by ;
Full pearly-gated, too, is she,
  Three gates on every side,
Which for the worn and weary hearts
  Stand alway open wide.

Her streets are of pure gold, as though
  Transparent glass one sees,
Her ways are ways of pleasantness
  And all her paths are peace ;
And in Love's city is no curse,
  No shadows darken there,
The Lamb, the light thereof, doth make
  All lustrous everywhere.

The clear Life-River through her midst
  In grateful fulness flows,
Upon whose banks the Tree of Life
  With healing leafage grows ;
Nor hunger there, nor pain of thirst,
  Love casteth out all fears,
And God most gently wipes away
  The traces of our tears.

O wondrous New Jerusalem,
  From Heaven thou art come down !
On earth thy firm foundations are,
  Here weareth Christ his crown ;
Here for the symbols of his reign
  We rightful search begin ;
O loveliest Christ, O Christliest Love,
  Thy kingdom is within !

Here is the radiant glory,

   And here the rapture song,

The multitudinous angels,

   The vast redeemèd throng ;

The pavement fair and golden,

   Life's River broad and pure,

Christ's true Jerusalem sounding

   Redemption's overture !

The Resurrection trumpet ! It

   Hath sounded o'er my soul,

Its loud reverberations

   Roll forth from pole to pole ;

The mountains rise in terror,

   The valleys bend in prayer ;

The sea grows hoarse with moaning,

   The skies with anger glare.

The Resurrection trumpet !   It
　　Hath sounded o'er the soul ;
Through all her mystic vastnesses
　　The solemn thunders roll ;
From out their long imprisonment
　　The waiting dead arise,
To hail the Master, marshalling
　　His armies in the skies !

Ah ! not with dread appear the dead
　　Before the Master now ;
Beneath his crown no darkling frown ;
　　Sweet mercy lights his brow ;
For this fair day have waited they
　　In dark confinement long :
Now burst they forth from tombs of earth ;
　　Now bursteth forth their song.

O throbbing Hopes of years gone by,

    Ye weak yet holy Cares,

O blushing, panting, fainting Loves,

    Ye sad yet sweet Despairs,

True Souls within my soul ye be,

    Nor need, nor shall ye die ;

Long-buried saints of God, arise,

    Redemption draweth nigh !

And now they rise, long-buried rise

    From out the tainted tomb ;

From deathful sin's enthralment spring

    To Paradise's bloom ;

Sown in corruption basest, rise

    In whiteness as the light ;

Dishonored, rise illustrious,

    From weakness rise to might !

Oh, ravishment unspeakable
    With which their Lord they greet ;
With Love's surprised bewilderment
    They cast them at his feet ;
No Day of Judgment grand and dread,
    No *dies iræ* this,
But grand, imposing vestibule
    To their immortal bliss.

The bliss of quick obedience
    To his low-whispered will,
The bliss of holy idleness
    When He shall bid, stand still ;
The rapture of a chieftain's soul
    When He to arms shall call,
Hope's jubilant expectancy
    Of triumph over all.

O Resurrection morning,

    Entrancing tearless eyes!

O chants of fairest angels,

    Thrilling these mystic skies!

Thou strange, unworldly world within–

    That Jesus died to save,

In thee no sigh nor moaning now,

    No melancholy grave!

Thou fair Jerusalem of God,

    Supernally away

Above our most adventurous thoughts;

    Thou art with us to day;

In human hearts hast thou thy throne,

    Here, Lord, thy servants be,

To stand before thy face, and do

    Thy will right loyally.

Here is the radiant glory,

  And here the rapture-song ;

Here multitudinous angels,

  And the redeemèd throng ;

The pavement fair and golden,

  The river broad and pure ;

The true Jerusalem swelling

  Redemption's overture !

VII.

Ay, now, thou dear Jerusalem,

  God bless and bless thee ever,

With crystal fulness flow thy peace

  As flows thy gentle river ;

Thy streets and temples hallowed be

  With joy and song unending ;

Thy sainted fears and prayers and hopes

  Before God's throne low bending.

But fear and pain steal o'er my soul,
　　My joy to grief gives birth ;
The clouds that glorify the sky
　　Cast shadows on the earth ;
Songs the Immortals sing, if touched
　　By mortal discord, jar,
And earthly incompletenesses
　　A heavenly vision mar !

O City, temple, song of God,
　　From Heaven thou art come down,
With all thy rich magnificence
　　And all thy just renown ;
There stood thy walls well builded, all
　　Immaculate thy white,
Thy hymns ne'er ununisonant,
　　Unmarrèd thy delight.

Lo! on the cragged mountain heights,
  And on the marshy plain,
Can Heaven's castellated. walls
  A safe foundation gain?
Can our earth-air so lowering,
  So light a song maintain?
Shall not its clearest crystalness
  The heavenly lustre stain?

Ah, well! there be wild storms that give
  A nobler close to-day,
Indignant lightnings thresh the skies
  To fright the plague away,
Mayhap some waters sweeter prove
  For trailing through the meadows,
God's light may all the choicer be
  For sifting through the shadows!

Songs of my soul! discordant
  Their notes may sometimes be;
Unversed the minstrel, broken
  The puzzled melody;
Untuned the harp and viol;
  But (fond conceit to me,)
If pleasing be this tuning,
  What shall the music be?

O Master-Builder, quarry from
  My heart the rock-hard part;
Nor mind the pain if Thou but gain
  Chance for thy perfect art;
The valleys fill, mountain and hill
  Smoothe down, and safe on them
Rear loftier walls and palaces
  Of the New Jerusalem.

O Master-Artist, these wild peaks .
   Convert to temple spires,
On all these swelling hills of pride
   Kindle thine altar fires ;
These pestilential fogs uplift
   Pure incense-clouds on high ;
And with what damps and darkens earth
   Incarnadine the sky.

O Master-Singer, frozen song
   This heart-world sure must be ;
Breathe Thou upon it, it shall melt
   To one soft symphony ;
The strange spell that enthralls it now
   Thou sure canst disenchant,
And blend into rich song the strains
   So sad, so dissonant.

Lord God, mountains and clouds and seas
    To thy grand choir belong,
Thy lightning like a gemmed baton
    Beats time for the thunder-song;
Rule Thou in this wild nature, Lord,
    These passion-tempests calm,
And from the myriad clang and jar
    Evoke the noble psalm.

Ay, as the night's deep darkness makes
    More radiant the dawn;
As life's most hallowed, hallowing joys
    Are oft from sorrows drawn;
As minor strains the noblest song's
    Rich pathos may improve:
Our shadowing sins may make the more
    Illustrious thy love.

The fractured glass shall daintily
   Caress the sunbeam white,
Teasing into a rainbow smile
   The frightened, trembling light ;
Lord, Thou canst use our brokenness
   To gem the heavenly wall,
And through our faults and frailties screen
   Transplendent grace o'er all.

Not less is thy true kingdom here
   Because of human weakness :
Not less thy joy in us because
   Our fall hath led to meekness ;
Our praise is not less grateful, Lord,
   Because well mixed with praying ;
Nor find we Welcome-Home less warm
   Because returned from straying !

Dear Christ, not in poor Palestine
    Poor signs of Thee we trace ;
Not through the boundless star-shine
    For semblance of thy face ;   [search
Not for a far-off earth-time wait
    Our Saviour to behold,
Nor gaze beyond the stream of death
    Through yonder gates of gold.

The stars be near, the times be here ;
    And walls all diamond-strewn ;
The myriad throng, the golden song,
    And the eternal throne ;
Here seraphim and cherubim
    Before Thee reverent bow ;
Lord Jesus, we too worship Thee,
    We see Thee here and now !

To our long yearning, waiting hearts
    Thou hast this word to say :
" He sees the Master's face who loves
    The Master to obey ;
My father and my mother they
    Who gladly do my will ;
They serve Me well who for my poor
    The cup of blessing fill ! "

Oh, sacred joy to us who long
    His absence have deplored,
To see in living human forms
    The kindred of our Lord !
O Servant-Master, make us such
    True servants to mankind,
That they grateful memorial
    Of Thee in us may find.

So search we, Lord, not for some rare
　　Far visions of thy face ;
In present loves and joys and toils
　　Let us thy spirit trace ;
In brave contentions for the right,
　　Forgivenesses of wrong,
The fears that hope, the tears that smile,
　　Weak lives by faith made strong.

How dreadful every place with God,
　　Solemn each soul with Him
Before whom on exalted throne
　　Bow wingèd cherubim !
Oh ! ours with reverence to treat
　　The heart where He abides,
And bless the world o'er which the Lord
　　With august grace presides !

Yes, Saviour dear, Thou art most near,
  When most afar we deem,
And all is right and full of light
  That dark and wrong doth seem.
Thou hast thy will when frowning ill
  Our doubting hearts affrights;
Ah, had we only better known
  Thy love's great depths and heights!

Jesus, the world, so wordly, is
  Yet very full of Thee;
Restless with the imprisoned God
  The tempest and the sea:
In dark and tortuous veins are hid
  Mountains of ancient light,
In human weakness part of God's
  Yet undeveloped right.

To them that love thy will, O Christ,

There is no lack of Thee ;

Only our deafness will not hear,

Our blindness will not see ;

Earth's discords are the surplus strains

That beat in wildness round ;

Her darkness, surplus light with which

Unseen stars strew the ground !

VIII.

I think of that brave instrument,*

Most wonderful, whereby

From all the harsh and Babel cries

That our sore senses try,

The listening ear may sort the strains

That best her fancy please,

Singling from sounds most clangorous

Harmonious symphonies.

* *The Silent Melodeon.*—See Appendix.

Amidst the city's din are heard
    The bells of Sabbath ringing,
And through the factory's buzz and hum
    The songs of children singing :
Through the deep solemn chimes of war
    The hymns of home are gliding ;
Behind resounding thunder-blasts
    The timid choirs are hiding.

Faith is that wondrous instrument
    Whereby the soul may hear
Amid the woes and wails of life
    The songs of hope and cheer ;
We stand among the myriad sounds
    That fill the troubled earth,
And ever choose the strains we will
    Of sadness or of mirth.

We sit beside the groaning sea
  Of human fear and sorrow,
And catch immortal symphonies
  From God's eternal Morrow ;
Within us fares the fearful fray
  Of many hosts contending,
Yet well we hear the victor-cries
  O'er contests grandly ending.

Oh! hoarse the shouts and wild the fray
  Where fight the good and ill,
And how shall we keep courage up
  With God so far, so still?
And human breasts are filled with dread,
  As, mingling in the din,
They wonder when the Lord shall bid
  Grace to o'ermaster sin.

God ! hear what dreadful wraths and
　　Threaten thy noblest plan ;　　[cries
What wicked powers and plots of hell !
　　What fateful schemes of man !
Huge Wrong stands ofttimes uppermost,
　　And Right lies humbled low ;
And to discouraged ones it seems
　　That Thou wilt have it so !

Great songs of God are fast inclosed
　　In the world-organ vast,
The winds sweep up the quivering pipes
　　In stormy, angry blast ;
But Faith sits at the organ-board,
　　And deftly strikes the keys,
'Tis weird, 'tis grand, how earthly reeds
　　Breathe heavenly melodies !

Blow slow, blow fast, thou maddened
 blast,
  Thou shalt but Christ-songs bring
To trusting minds! Blow, Winter winds,
  Blow hard—ye speed the Spring,
Wild hurricanes, the tender strains
  Of love Faith makes ye blow;
As though the angels, strong and strange,
  Hosannas flung below.

Give me the ear, my God, to hear
  The songs the angels sing me,
Give me the eye that shall descry
  With joy the joys they bring me!
To my poor heart the power impart
  To know that Thou art near me;
And let Love listen to the Christ
  Who longs with love to cheer me.

Oh, for the ear that hearkening

    In stillness rapt and holy,

Misses no undertone of song

    Howe'er so soft and lowly ;

The ear that notes the mystic psalms

    The mystic choirs are singing ;

God louder in his silences

    Than clouds when thunders flinging !

Oh, for the eye that out beyond

    The stars spies others gleaming,

That scans the Unbeheld as real,

    The Seen as only seeming ;

The eye that earthly blindness helps

    To spiritual seeing,

And deep within the inmost finds

    The richer, fuller being !

Through all thy myriad crowding worlds,
   In vain I search for Thee,
Till by thy clearer vision Thou
   Searchest and savest me ;
Then, Master, I essay no more
   To find the holy spot
Where dwellest Thou ; I wondering ask,
   Where shall I find Thee not ?

Dear Christ, in this unworthy heart
   Dwell with celestial grace,
Let the whole world be splendent with
   The glory of thy face ;
While we below far upward press
   Our arduous, ardent way,   [down,
Thy heavens, O Lord of Hosts, bring
   And here thy power display !

Here be the radiant glory,

    And here the rapture-song,

Here multitudinous angels,

    And the full-ransomed throng ;

The City fair and golden,

    Life's River, broad and pure ;

Thy New Jerusalem, sounding

    Redemption's Overture !

A·PPEND1X.

Page 51.—"I THINK OF THAT BRAVE INSTRU-
MENT."

EVER since I read of *The Silent Melodeon* I
have loved to think of it as a striking illustration
of the manner in which the trusting, loving spirit
will hear songs of Christ in all possible discords
and tumults of the world ; and have ventured so
to employ it here. For a full account of this
peculiar instrument, see *Appleton's Annual
Cyclopædia for* 1868, *p.* 463, from which I ab-
stract and condense the following :

" *The Silent Melodeon.*—In 1868, M. Daguin,
a French physician, invented the analyzing cor-
net by which, out of a confused body of sound,
of many different notes, he could separate and
make audible by itself alone any particular note
at pleasure. This instrument consists of several
tubes, opening and shutting together, like those
of a telescope. By varying the length of the
instrument, the length and volume of the column
of inclosed air will also be changed to an equal
extent. In this way, by lengthening and shorten-
ing the cornet, certain notes are emphasized, and
heard separately from the others.

"In The Silent Melodeon the volume of the column of air is not changed as in the cornet, but remains constantly the same; and the sound is modulated through holes in the tube, which are opened and shut by the fingers, like a flute. The tube is bell-mouthed at one end, and closed at the other with a perforated button which in use is pressed against the ear. By varying the order of opening the holes, the desired note is separated from the other mingling sounds, and is distinctly and separately heard.

"With this instrument all the notes of the gamut can be made audible, with no other base than the confused body of mingling sounds. A tune can be played, heard by no one but the person using the instrument. He will hear a melody, audible only to himself, through an instrument which makes no sound. He selects the notes he chooses. M. Daguin has named this instrument The Silent Melodeon, because it plays a tune without creating a sound.

"One of these, a three-holed instrument on which a perfect major chord can be sounded, has been presented by M. Daguin to the Academy. For the purpose of producing what corresponds to double-vision, he has made use of two instruments, one at each ear. The separate notes, diverse in sound, but equal in vibration, seem one."

Lightning Source UK Ltd.
Milton Keynes UK
UKHW010014230119
336029UK00006B/134/P